FARMER'S MARKET

Recipes

FRESH FOOD
FRESH IDEAS

Publications International, Ltd.

Front cover photography by Peter Ross Studio, Chicago.

Pictured on the front cover: Chicken Caesar *(page 52).*
Pictured on the back cover *(clockwise from top left):* Fresh Vegetable Basil Medley *(page 54)* and Mapley Berry Shortcake *(page 68).*

ISBN: 0-7853-2388-0

Manufactured in U.S.A.

8   7   6   5   4   3   2   1

Microwave Cooking: Microwave ovens vary in wattage. Use the cooking times as guidelines and check for doneness before adding more time.

FARMER'S MARKET

Recipes

FRESH FOOD
FRESH IDEAS

Summertime Starters

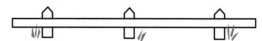

Marinated Tomatoes & Mozzarella

1 medium bunch fresh
  basil leaves, divided
1 pound Italian tomatoes,
  sliced
½ pound fresh packed
  buffalo mozzarella
  cheese, sliced
½ cup LAWRY'S® Red
  Wine Vinaigrette with
  Cabernet Sauvignon
½ teaspoon LAWRY'S®
  Seasoned Pepper
½ teaspoon LAWRY'S®
  Garlic Powder with
  Parsley

Divide basil in half; reserve
one half for garnish. Chop
remaining basil leaves; set
aside. In shallow dish, place
tomato and cheese slices.
Combine all remaining
ingredients except reserved
whole and chopped basil
leaves; pour mixture over
tomatoes and cheese. Cover
and refrigerate at least
30 minutes. To serve, arrange
tomato and cheese slices on
serving plate. Sprinkle with
chopped basil leaves. Garnish
with reserved whole basil
leaves.

Makes 4 to 6 servings

**Marinated Tomatoes &
Mozzarella**

Thai Chicken Pizza

- 2 boneless skinless
  chicken breast halves
  (½ pound)
- 2 teaspoons Thai
  seasoning
- 2 tablespoons pineapple
  juice
- 1 tablespoon peanut
  butter
- 1 tablespoon oyster sauce
- 1 teaspoon Thai chili
  paste*
- 2 (10-inch) flour tortillas
- ½ cup shredded carrot
- ½ cup sliced green onions
- ½ cup red bell pepper
  slices
- ¼ cup chopped cilantro
- ½ cup (2 ounces) shredded
  mozzarella cheese

Thai chili paste is available at some larger supermarkets and at Asian markets.

1. Preheat oven to 400°F. Cut chicken breasts crosswise into thin slices, each about 1½×½ inch. Sprinkle with Thai seasoning. Let stand 5 minutes. Spray large nonstick skillet with cooking spray; heat over medium heat until hot. Add chicken; cook and stir 3 minutes or until chicken is lightly browned and no longer pink in center.

Thai Chicken Pizza

2. Combine pineapple juice, peanut butter, oyster sauce and chili paste in small bowl until smooth.

3. Place tortillas on baking sheets. Spread peanut butter mixture over tortillas. Divide chicken, carrot, green onions, bell pepper and cilantro evenly among tortillas. Sprinkle with cheese. Bake 5 minutes or until tortillas are crisp and cheese is melted. Cut into wedges.
Makes 4 servings

Roasted Spice Gazpacho

     3 large tomatoes, halved and cored
     1 medium zucchini, cut lengthwise into ½-inch-thick slices
     1 medium onion, cut into ½-inch-thick slices
     1 medium green bell pepper, halved and seeded
     3 tablespoons olive oil, divided
    1½ teaspoons ground cumin
    1½ teaspoons ground coriander
     1 teaspoon garlic powder
     2 cups tomato juice
     ½ teaspoon salt

Prepare grill or preheat broiler. Arrange vegetables in single layer on grill or rack of broiler pan; brush with 1 tablespoon oil. Grill 4 to 5 inches from heat until tender, about 10 minutes, turning and brushing with 1 tablespoon oil after 5 minutes. Place vegetables on cutting board; cool slightly.

Meanwhile, heat remaining 1 tablespoon oil in small saucepan over medium-low heat; add cumin, coriander and garlic powder. Cook 1 to 2 minutes or until fragrant, stirring occasionally. Coarsely chop vegetables and place in large bowl; stir in spice mixture, tomato juice and salt. Cover and refrigerate about 4 hours or until chilled. Serve with dollop of plain yogurt or sour cream and lime wedges, if desired.   *Makes 6 cups*

*Favorite recipe from **American Spice Trade Association***

Herbed Croutons with Savory Bruschetta

½ cup regular or reduced fat mayonnaise
¼ cup FRENCH'S® Dijon Mustard
1 tablespoon finely chopped green onion
1 clove garlic, minced
¾ teaspoon dried oregano leaves
1 long thin loaf (18 inches) French bread, cut crosswise into ½-inch-thick slices
Savory Bruschetta (recipe follows)

Combine mayonnaise, mustard, onion, garlic and oregano in small bowl; mix well. Spread herbed mixture on one side of each slice of bread.

Place bread, spread sides up, on grid. Grill over medium-low coals 1 minute or until lightly toasted. Spoon Savory Bruschetta onto Herbed Croutons. Serve warm.
Makes 6 appetizer servings

Prep Time: 10 minutes
Cook Time: 1 minute

Tip: Leftover croutons may be served with dips or cut up and served in salads.

Savory Bruschetta

1 pound ripe plum tomatoes, cored, seeded and chopped
1 cup finely chopped fennel bulb or celery
¼ cup chopped fresh basil leaves
3 tablespoons FRENCH'S® Dijon Mustard
3 tablespoons olive oil
3 tablespoons balsamic vinegar
2 cloves garlic, minced
½ teaspoon salt

Combine ingredients in medium bowl; toss well to mix evenly. *Makes 3 cups*

Prep Time: 15 minutes

Herbed Croutons with Savory Bruschetta

10

Pear-Pepper Salsa

2 fresh California Bartlett
    pears, peeled, cored
    and diced (about
    2½ cups)
⅓ cup diced red bell
    pepper
⅓ cup golden raisins
2 green onions, thinly
    sliced
1 fresh jalapeño pepper,
    minced *or*
    1 tablespoon canned
    diced jalapeño
    peppers
1 tablespoon white wine
    vinegar
2 teaspoons minced fresh
    ginger *or* ½ teaspoon
    ground ginger
8 fresh flour tortillas,
    quartered or cut into
    strips, warmed

Combine all ingredients except
tortillas in medium bowl.
Cover and refrigerate. Spoon
onto tortillas.

Makes about 3 cups

Serving Suggestion: Makes a
delicious low-calorie topping
for grilled chicken, pork or
fish.

*Favorite recipe from **California Tree
Fruit Agreement***

Fresh Peach Salsa

2 fresh California
    peaches, diced
    (about 1⅓ cups)
2 plums, diced (about
    ⅔ cup)
⅓ cup raisins
¼ cup diced red onion
1 to 2 tablespoons lemon
    juice
1 tablespoon chopped
    fresh mint
8 fresh flour tortillas,
    quartered or cut into
    strips, warmed

Combine all ingredients except
tortillas in medium bowl.
Cover and refrigerate. Spoon
onto tortillas.

Makes about 3 cups

Tip: Salsa is best if prepared
one day ahead.

*Favorite recipe from **California Tree
Fruit Agreement***

Top to bottom:
**Fresh Peach Salsa,
Pear-Pepper Salsa and
Mint-Nectarine Salsa
(page 15)**

Cold Asparagus with Lemon-Mustard Dressing

12 fresh asparagus spears
2 tablespoons fat-free mayonnaise
1 tablespoon sweet brown mustard
1 tablespoon fresh lemon juice
1 teaspoon grated lemon peel, divided

1. Steam asparagus until crisp-tender and bright green; immediately drain and run under cold water. Cover and refrigerate until chilled.

2. Combine mayonnaise, mustard and lemon juice in small bowl; blend well. Stir in ½ teaspoon lemon peel; set aside.

3. Divide asparagus between 2 plates. Spoon 2 tablespoons dressing over top of each serving; sprinkle each with ¼ teaspoon lemon peel. Garnish with carrot strips and edible flowers, such as pansies, violets or nasturtiums, if desired. *Makes 2 appetizer servings*

Cold Asparagus with Lemon-Mustard Dressing

Mint-Nectarine Salsa

    **2 fresh California
        nectarines, chopped
1½ tablespoons chopped
        fresh mint
  1 tablespoon lemon juice
  8 fresh flour tortillas,
        quartered or cut into
        strips, warmed**

Combine nectarines, mint and
lemon juice in small bowl.
Cover and refrigerate. Spoon
onto tortillas.

Makes about 1½ cups

*Favorite recipe from **California Tree
Fruit Agreement***

Italian Flat Bread

**2½ to 3 cups all-purpose
      flour
  1 package RED STAR®
      Active Dry Yeast or
      QUICK•RISE™ Yeast
  1 tablespoon sugar
  1 teaspoon salt
  1 cup very warm water
      (120° to 130°F)
  1 tablespoon olive oil
    Toppings, such as sun-
      dried tomatoes,
      grilled green pepper
      slices, sautéed onion
      rings, fresh and dried
      herbs of any
      combination, grated
      hard cheese (optional)**

In large mixer bowl, combine
1½ cups flour, yeast, sugar and
salt; mix well. Add water and
oil to flour mixture. Blend at
low speed until moistened; beat
3 minutes at medium speed. By
hand, gradually stir in enough
remaining flour to make a firm
dough. Knead on floured
surface 5 to 8 minutes. Place in
greased bowl, turning to grease
top. Cover; let rise in warm
place about 20 minutes.

Turn dough onto lightly
floured surface; punch down to
remove air bubbles. Shape
dough into a ball; place on
greased cookie sheet. Flatten
dough into 14-inch circle. With
table knife, cut circle in dough
about 1 inch from edge, cutting
almost through to cookie
sheet. Prick center with fork.
Cover; let rise about
15 minutes. Brush with
additional olive oil and
sprinkle with desired toppings.
Bake in preheated 375°F oven
25 to 30 minutes or until
golden brown. Remove from
cookie sheet to cool. Serve
warm or cold.

Makes 1 (14-inch) flat bread

Corn and Tomato Chowder

1½ cups peeled and diced
    plum tomatoes
¾ teaspoon salt, divided
2 ears corn, husks
    removed
1 tablespoon margarine
½ cup finely chopped
    shallots
1 clove garlic, minced
1 can (12 ounces)
    evaporated skimmed
    milk
1 cup chicken broth
1 tablespoon finely
    chopped fresh sage *or*
    1 teaspoon rubbed
    sage
¼ teaspoon pepper
1 tablespoon cornstarch
2 tablespoons cold water

1. Place tomatoes in nonmetal colander over bowl. Sprinkle ½ teaspoon salt on top; toss to mix well. Allow tomatoes to drain at least 1 hour.

2. Meanwhile, cut corn kernels off the cobs into small bowl. Scrape cobs with dull side of knife to extract liquid from cobs into same bowl; set aside. Discard 1 cob; break remaining cob in half.

3. Heat margarine in heavy medium saucepan over medium-high heat until melted and bubbly. Add shallots and garlic; reduce heat to low. Cover and cook about 5 minutes or until shallots are soft and translucent. Add milk, broth, sage, pepper and reserved corn cob halves. Bring to a boil over high heat. Reduce heat to low; simmer, uncovered, 10 minutes. Remove and discard cob halves.

4. Add corn with liquid; return to a boil over medium-high heat. Reduce heat to low; simmer, uncovered, 15 minutes more. Dissolve cornstarch in water; add to chowder, mixing well. Stir until thickened. Remove from heat; stir in drained tomatoes and remaining ¼ teaspoon salt. Spoon into bowls. Garnish with additional fresh sage, if desired.

Makes 6 appetizer servings

Corn and Tomato Chowder

Garden Fresh Salads

Avocado-Melon Salad with Strawberry Vinaigrette

Strawberry Vinaigrette
(recipe follows)
2 avocados, pitted, peeled
and sliced
2 cups cantaloupe or
Crenshaw melon balls
1 cup fresh strawberry
slices
1 bunch watercress,
trimmed

Prepare Strawberry
Vinaigrette. Arrange avocados,
melon and strawberries on
salad plates. Arrange
watercress around fruit. Serve
with dressing.
Makes 4 servings

Strawberry Vinaigrette

1 cup fresh strawberry
slices
3 tablespoons vegetable
oil
2 tablespoons lime juice
2 tablespoons red wine
vinegar
1 teaspoon sugar

Combine ingredients in
blender or food processor.
Cover; blend until smooth.
Strain dressing through
fine-meshed sieve. Cover; chill.
Makes about ½ cup

**Avocado-Melon Salad with
Strawberry Vinaigrette**

Pasta Garden Salad

1 package (16 ounces) ridged mostaccioli, ziti or medium shell macaroni, uncooked
4 cups assorted cut-up vegetables, such as green beans, broccoli flowerets, red and yellow pepper strips, sliced yellow squash and zucchini
1 cup sliced pitted ripe olives
½ cup (2 ounces) grated Parmesan cheese
½ cup chopped fresh parsley (optional)
1 cup prepared GOOD SEASONS® Italian Salad Dressing

PREPARE pasta as directed on package; drain. Rinse with cold water; drain.

MIX pasta, vegetables, olives, cheese and parsley in large bowl. Add dressing; toss to coat.

SERVE immediately or refrigerate until ready to serve.
Makes 8 servings

Prep Time: 25 minutes

Pasta Garden Salad

Mixed Vegetable and Noodle Salad with Sesame Dressing

2 cups sliced green or napa cabbage

1½ cups broccoli florets, blanched and cooled

1 cup trimmed snow peas, blanched and cooled

½ cup thinly sliced cucumber

⅓ cup toasted DIAMOND® Walnuts, coarsely chopped

Sesame Dressing (recipe follows)

1 package (8 ounces) angel hair, linguine or vermicelli noodles, cooked according to package directions, drained and cooled

In bowl, combine vegetables and walnuts; toss with half of dressing. Set aside. In another bowl, toss noodles with remaining dressing. To serve, top noodles with vegetable mixture. *Makes 4 servings*

Sesame Dressing: In bowl, whisk together 6 tablespoons rice wine vinegar, 3 tablespoons low-sodium soy sauce, ¼ cup chopped fresh cilantro or parsley, 5 cloves minced garlic, 3 teaspoons *each* sesame oil and honey and ¼ teaspoon red pepper flakes.

Country Orchard Salad with Raspberry Walnut Dressing

2 medium pears, cored and sliced

2 medium peaches, pitted and sliced

8 ounces seedless grapes, cut into clusters

2 medium kiwifruit, peeled and sliced

1 large banana, sliced

8 green leaf lettuce leaves

3 tablespoons toasted DIAMOND® Walnuts, coarsely chopped

Raspberry Walnut Dressing (recipe follows)

To serve, arrange fruit on lettuce-lined salad plates. Sprinkle with walnuts and drizzle with dressing; serve immediately.

Makes 4 servings

Raspberry Walnut Dressing: In electric blender, combine 1 cup fresh or loose-pack thawed frozen raspberries, ½ cup undiluted frozen apple juice concentrate and 2 tablespoons white wine vinegar or balsamic vinegar; blend until smooth. Strain to remove seeds. Stir in ⅓ cup toasted Diamond® Walnuts, chopped.

Kielbasa Tomato Salad

1 pound BOB EVANS
   FARMS® Kielbasa
   Sausage
1 pound tomatoes, cut
   into wedges
1 large red onion,
   chopped
1 red bell pepper, chopped
1 yellow bell pepper,
   chopped
3 green onions with tops,
   cut into ½-inch pieces
½ cup chopped fresh
   parsley
⅓ cup balsamic vinegar
2 teaspoons salt
1 teaspoon chopped fresh
   rosemary leaves
1 teaspoon chopped fresh
   thyme
1 teaspoon black pepper
½ cup olive oil
   Fresh rosemary sprig
   (optional)

Cut kielbasa into ½-inch
rounds; place in medium
skillet. Cook over medium heat
until browned, turning
occasionally. Remove sausage
to large glass bowl. Add
tomatoes, red onion, bell
peppers and green onions to
sausage; toss lightly. Combine
all remaining ingredients
except oil and rosemary sprig
in small bowl. Whisk in oil
gradually until well blended.

Pour over sausage mixture;
cover and refrigerate 2 hours
or until chilled. Garnish with
rosemary sprig, if desired.
Serve cold. Refrigerate
leftovers.
   Makes 8 side-dish servings

Wisconsin Provolone and Sweet Pepper Slaw

3 cups green cabbage,
   shredded
2 cups (8 ounces) cubed
   Wisconsin Provolone
   cheese
1 cup shredded red
   cabbage
1 cup coarsely chopped
   assorted bell peppers
   (red, yellow, green
   and/or orange)
¾ cup bottled Caesar
   salad dressing
⅓ cup green onions, sliced

Combine all ingredients in
large bowl; mix well. Cover and
refrigerate 1 hour to blend
flavors. Toss before serving.
   Makes 6 to 8 servings

*Favorite recipe from **Wisconsin Milk
Marketing Board***

Kielbasa Tomato Salad

Roasted Pepper and Avocado Salad

Roasted Pepper and Avocado Salad

2 red bell peppers
2 orange bell peppers
2 yellow bell peppers
2 ripe avocados, halved, pitted and peeled
3 shallots, thinly sliced
¼ cup FILIPPO BERIO® Extra Virgin Olive Oil
1 clove garlic, crushed
Finely grated peel and juice of 1 lemon
Salt and freshly ground black pepper

Place bell peppers on baking sheet. Broil, 4 to 5 inches from heat, 5 minutes on each side or until entire surface of each bell pepper is blistered and blackened slightly. Place bell peppers in paper bag. Close bag; cool 15 to 20 minutes. Cut around cores of bell peppers; twist and remove. Cut bell peppers lengthwise in half. Peel off skin with paring knife; rinse under cold water to remove seeds. Slice bell peppers into ½-inch-thick strips; place in shallow dish. Cut avocados into ¼-inch-thick slices; add to bell peppers. Sprinkle with shallots.

In small bowl, whisk together olive oil, garlic, lemon peel and juice. Pour over bell pepper mixture. Cover; refrigerate at least 1 hour before serving. Season to taste with salt and black pepper.

Makes 6 servings

Mixed Green Salad with Walnuts, Sun-Dried Tomatoes and Gorgonzola

8 cups torn salad greens of your choice *or* 2 bags (7 ounces each) prepared mixed salad greens
½ cup toasted DIAMOND® Walnuts, coarsely chopped
½ cup sun-dried tomatoes, snipped into quarters, reconstituted according to package directions and drained
⅓ cup crumbled Gorgonzola cheese
Lemon-Dijon Vinaigrette (recipe follows)

In salad bowl, gently toss all ingredients; serve immediately.

Makes 4 servings

Lemon-Dijon Vinaigrette: In bowl, whisk together ¼ cup olive oil, 2 tablespoons red wine vinegar, 2 teaspoons Dijon mustard, 1½ teaspoons sugar, grated peel of 1 lemon, 1 clove minced garlic and ¼ teaspoon *each* salt and pepper.

Confetti Wild Rice Salad

1 package (6 ounces) white and wild rice mix
1 *each* red and yellow bell pepper, seeded and chopped
¼ cup finely chopped red onion
¼ cup minced fresh parsley
¼ cup minced fresh basil leaves
⅓ cup FRENCH'S® Dijon Mustard
¼ cup olive oil
¼ cup red wine vinegar

Prepare rice according to package directions; cool completely.

Place rice in large bowl. Add peppers, onion, parsley and basil. Combine mustard, oil and vinegar in small bowl; mix well. Pour over rice and vegetables; toss well to coat evenly. Cover and refrigerate 1 hour before serving. Garnish as desired.

Makes 8 side-dish servings

Prep Time: 20 minutes
Cook Time: 20 minutes
Chill Time: 1 hour

Fruit Salad with Orange Poppy Seed Dressing

¼ cup orange juice
3 tablespoons cider vinegar
3 tablespoons FRENCH'S® Dijon Mustard
2 tablespoons honey
1 tablespoon FRENCH'S® Worcestershire Sauce
1 teaspoon grated orange peel
½ teaspoon salt
½ cup canola or corn oil
1 tablespoon poppy seeds
6 cups fruit: such as orange segments; cantaloupe, watermelon and/or honeydew melon balls; blueberries; blackberries; grapes; star fruit and/or strawberry slices; nectarine wedges
Lettuce leaves

To prepare dressing, place orange juice, vinegar, mustard, honey, Worcestershire, orange peel and salt in food processor or blender. Cover and process until well blended. Gradually add oil in steady stream, processing until very smooth. Stir in poppy seeds.

Arrange fruit on lettuce leaves on large platter. Spoon dressing over fruit just before serving.
Makes 6 side-dish servings (about 1½ cups dressing)

Prep Time: 40 minutes

Marinated Summer Salad

4 medium zucchini, diced
1 can (8 ounces) garbanzo beans, drained
½ cup chopped red onion
1 medium tomato, diced
1 can (2¼ ounces) sliced pitted ripe olives, drained
¾ cup LAWRY'S® Herb and Garlic Marinade with Lemon Juice

In large bowl, combine all ingredients; toss lightly. Cover. Refrigerate at least 30 minutes. Serve and garnish as desired.
Makes 4 servings

Presentation: Serve on lettuce-covered platter as a side dish with sandwiches or your favorite chicken recipe.

Fruit Salad with Orange Poppy Seed Dressing

Farmer's Market Salad

2 cups cucumber chunks
2 cups thickly sliced
    celery
2 cups pepper chunks
2 cups halved cherry
    tomatoes
1 cup sliced radishes
1 cup red onion chunks
1 cup prepared GOOD
    SEASONS® Zesty
    Herb Salad Dressing
    Mix for Fat Free
    Dressing or GOOD
    SEASONS® Italian
    Salad Dressing Mix
    for Fat Free Dressing*

*For a change of pace, experiment with
different combinations of vinegars and
oils when preparing your favorite
GOOD SEASONS® flavor.*

MIX vegetables in large bowl.
Add dressing; toss to mix well.
Refrigerate at least 2 hours,
stirring occasionally.

Makes 10 cups

Prep Time: 10 minutes plus
refrigerating.

Vinegar Variations: Try
apple cider, red wine, balsamic,
raspberry or tarragon vinegar.
Or, use fresh lemon, orange,
grapefruit, lime or tomato juice
instead of vinegar.

Oil Options: Use vegetable,
canola, corn, safflower or olive
oil. (With olive oil, let
refrigerated dressing reach
room temperature before
serving.)

Spinach and Strawberry Salad with Wisconsin Gouda

¼ cup orange juice
 3 tablespoons vegetable
    oil
 1 tablespoon honey
 1 teaspoon grated orange
    peel
¼ teaspoon garlic salt
⅛ teaspoon paprika
 4 cups spinach leaves
 1 pint strawberries,
    stemmed and halved
 1 cup (4 ounces)
    Wisconsin Gouda
    cheese, cubed
½ cup pecan or walnut
    halves

Combine orange juice, oil,
honey, orange peel, garlic salt
and paprika in small container
with tight lid; shake well.

Toss spinach leaves,
strawberries, cheese and nuts
with dressing in large salad
bowl. Refrigerate or serve
immediately.

Makes 6 servings

Farmer's Market Salad

Pasta Pesto Salad

Pasta Salad

8 ounces three-color
    rotini pasta
3 small bell peppers,
    seeded and cut into
    thin strips
1 pint cherry tomatoes,
    stemmed and halved
6 ounces (1 block)
    ALPINE LACE® Fat
    Free Pasteurized
    Process Skim Milk
    Cheese Product—For
    Mozzarella Lovers,
    cut into ½-inch cubes
1 cup thin carrot circles
1 cup thin strips red
    onion
1 cup slivered fresh basil

Spicy Dressing

½ cup (2 ounces) shredded
    ALPINE LACE® Fat
    Free Pasteurized
    Process Skim Milk
    Cheese Product—For
    Parmesan Lovers
⅓ cup packed parsley
⅓ cup extra virgin olive oil
⅓ cup red wine vinegar
2 large cloves garlic
1 tablespoon whole-grain
    Dijon mustard
¾ teaspoon black pepper
½ teaspoon salt

1. To make the Pasta Salad: Cook the pasta according to package directions until al dente. Drain in a colander, rinse under cold water and drain again. Place the pasta in a large shallow pasta bowl and toss with the remaining salad ingredients.

2. To make the Spicy Dressing: In a food processor or blender, process all of the dressing ingredients for 30 seconds or until well blended.

3. Drizzle the dressing on the salad and toss to mix well. Cover with plastic wrap and refrigerate for 1 hour so the flavors can blend, or let stand at room temperature for 1 hour.

Makes 12 side-dish or
6 main-dish servings

Pasta Pesto Salad

Marinated Tomato Salad

Marinade

 1½ cups tarragon or white wine vinegar
 ½ teaspoon salt
 ¼ cup finely chopped shallots
 2 tablespoons finely chopped chives
 2 tablespoons fresh lemon juice
 ¼ teaspoon ground white pepper
 2 tablespoons extra virgin olive oil

Salad

 6 plum tomatoes, quartered vertically
 2 large yellow tomatoes, sliced horizontally into ½-inch slices
 16 red cherry tomatoes, halved vertically
 16 small yellow pear tomatoes, halved vertically

1. To prepare Marinade, combine vinegar and salt in large bowl; stir until salt is completely dissolved. Add shallots, chives, lemon juice and white pepper; mix well. Slowly whisk in oil until well blended.

2. Add tomatoes to marinade; toss well. Cover and let stand at room temperature 2 to 3 hours.

3. To serve, place 3 plum tomato quarters on each of 8 salad plates. Add 2 slices yellow tomato, 4 cherry tomato halves and 4 pear tomato halves. Garnish each plate with sunflower sprouts, if desired. (Or, place all marinated tomatoes on large serving plate.)

Makes 8 servings

Marinated Tomato Salad

Market Day Main Dishes

Red Snapper Vera Cruz

4 red snapper fillets
    (1 pound)
¼ cup fresh lime juice
1 tablespoon fresh lemon
    juice
1 teaspoon chili powder
4 green onions with
    4 inches of tops, sliced
    in ½-inch lengths
1 tomato, coarsely
    chopped
½ cup chopped Anaheim
    or green bell pepper
½ cup chopped red bell
    pepper

1. Place red snapper in shallow microwavable baking dish. Combine lime juice, lemon juice and chili powder. Pour over snapper. Marinate 10 minutes, turning once or twice.

2. Sprinkle onions, tomato and peppers over snapper. Cover dish loosely with plastic wrap. Microwave at HIGH 6 minutes or just until snapper flakes in center, rotating dish every 2 minutes. Let stand, covered, 4 minutes before serving.

Makes 4 servings

Red Snapper Vera Cruz

34

Roasted Vegetables with Fettuccine

2 pounds assorted fresh
  vegetables*
1 envelope LIPTON®
  Recipe Secrets®
  Golden Herb with
  Lemon Soup Mix**
3 tablespoons olive or
  vegetable oil
½ cup light cream,
  whipping or heavy
  cream or half-and-
  half
¼ cup grated Parmesan
  cheese
8 ounces fettuccine or
  linguine, cooked and
  drained

*Try red, green or yellow bell peppers, zucchini, yellow squash, red onion or eggplant, cut into 1-inch chunks.

**Also terrific with Lipton® Recipe Secrets® Savory Herb with Garlic or Fiesta Herb with Red Pepper.

Preheat oven to 450°F. In large plastic bag or bowl, combine vegetables, golden herb with lemon soup mix and oil. Close bag and shake, or toss in bowl until vegetables are evenly coated. In 13×9-inch baking pan, arrange vegetables; discard bag.

Bake uncovered 20 minutes or until vegetables are tender, stirring once. Stir in light cream and cheese until evenly coated. Toss with pasta. Serve, if desired, with additional Parmesan and pepper.

Makes about 2 main-dish or 4 side-dish servings

Chicken with Zucchini and Tomatoes

4 broiler-fryer chicken
  breast halves, skinned
2 tablespoons olive oil
2 small zucchini, cut in
  ¼-inch slices
1 can (14½ ounces) stewed
  tomatoes
½ teaspoon Italian
  seasoning
Salt and pepper to taste

Heat oil in large skillet to medium-high temperature. Add chicken and cook, turning, 10 minutes or until brown on both sides. Drain off excess fat. Add zucchini, tomatoes, Italian seasoning, salt and pepper. Reduce heat to medium-low; cover and cook about 20 minutes or until chicken and zucchini are fork-tender.

Makes 4 servings

*Favorite recipe from **Delmarva Poultry Industry, Inc.***

Roasted Vegetables with Fettuccine

Pepper Lovers' Pasta

1 (15-ounce) package
   BUCKEYE'S®
   Evergreen pasta*
1 *each* red, green and
   yellow bell pepper,
   thinly sliced
1 bunch leeks, cleaned
   and thinly sliced
¼ cup olive oil
3 ounces sun-dried
   tomatoes, sliced and
   puréed in blender or
   food processor
2 teaspoons minced garlic
2 teaspoons dried
   oregano
1 teaspoon dried basil
1 teaspoon dried thyme
1 teaspoon salt
¼ teaspoon black pepper

Cook pasta according to package directions until al dente. Sauté bell peppers and leeks in olive oil in large skillet until soft but still firm. Stir in puréed tomatoes, garlic, oregano, basil, thyme, salt, black pepper and drained pasta; toss to combine. Serve warm with additional black pepper.

Makes 4 to 6 servings

Call toll-free number (1-800-449-2121) to order shaped pasta.

Pepper Lovers' Pasta

Cantonese Tomato Beef

1 small beef flank steak
   or filet mignon tail
   (about 1 pound)
2 tablespoons soy sauce
2 tablespoons sesame oil,
   divided
1 tablespoon plus
   1 teaspoon
   cornstarch, divided
1 pound fresh Chinese-
   style thin wheat
   noodles *or* 12 ounces
   dry spaghetti
3 small onions (about
   7 ounces), peeled
2 pounds ripe tomatoes
   (5 large), cored
1 cup beef broth
2 tablespoons brown
   sugar
1 tablespoon cider
   vinegar
2 tablespoons vegetable
   oil, divided
1 tablespoon minced fresh
   ginger
1 green onion with tops,
   diagonally cut into
   thin slices
  Edible flowers, such as
   nasturtiums, for
   garnish

1. Trim fat from beef; discard. Cut beef lengthwise into 2 strips; cut across the grain into ¼-inch-thick slices (about 2 inches long).

2. Combine soy sauce, 1 tablespoon sesame oil and 1 teaspoon cornstarch in large bowl; mix well. Add beef slices and toss to coat. Set aside to marinate.

3. Cook noodles according to package directions *just* until tender. Meanwhile, cut each onion into 8 wedges, then cut each tomato into 8 wedges; set aside.

4. Combine broth, brown sugar, remaining 1 tablespoon cornstarch and vinegar in small bowl; mix well. Set aside.

5. Drain cooked noodles in colander and return to stockpot. Add remaining 1 tablespoon sesame oil; toss until well mixed. Set aside and keep warm.

continued on page 40

*Cantonese Tomato Beef,
continued*

6. Heat wok over high heat 1 minute or until hot. Drizzle 1 tablespoon vegetable oil into wok and heat 30 seconds. Add ginger and stir-fry about 30 seconds or until fragrant. Add beef mixture and stir-fry 5 minutes or until lightly browned. Remove beef and ginger to bowl and set aside. Reduce heat to medium.

7. Add remaining 1 tablespoon vegetable oil to wok. Add onion wedges; cook and stir about 2 minutes or until wilted. Stir in half of tomato wedges. Stir broth mixture and add to wok. Cook and stir until liquid boils and thickens.

8. Return beef and any juices to wok. Add remaining tomato wedges; cook and stir until heated through. Place cooked noodles in shallow serving bowl. Spoon tomato-beef mixture over noodles. Sprinkle with green onion. Garnish, if desired.   *Makes 4 servings*

Summer Chicken & Squash

**1 cup WISH-BONE®
    Italian Dressing***
**⅓ cup grated Parmesan
    cheese**
**4 boneless, skinless
    chicken breast halves
    (about 1¼ pounds)**
**2 medium zucchini or
    yellow squash,
    quartered**

*Also terrific with Wish-Bone® Robusto Italian, Lite Italian or Fat Free Italian Dressing.

• For marinade, blend Italian Dressing with cheese. In large, shallow nonaluminum baking dish or plastic bag, pour ¾ cup of the marinade over chicken and zucchini; turn to coat. Cover, or close bag, and marinate in refrigerator, turning occasionally, up to 3 hours. Refrigerate remaining ½ cup marinade.

• Remove chicken and zucchini from marinade; discard marinade. Grill or broil chicken and zucchini, turning and brushing frequently with refrigerated marinade, until chicken is no longer pink.
      Makes 4 servings

Cantonese Tomato Beef

Tomato, Basil & Broccoli Chicken

- 4 skinless, boneless chicken breast halves
- Salt and pepper (optional)
- 2 tablespoons margarine or butter
- 1 package (6.9 ounces) RICE-A-RONI® Chicken Flavor
- 1 teaspoon dried basil
- 2 cups broccoli flowerets
- 1 medium tomato, seeded, chopped
- 1 cup (4 ounces) shredded mozzarella cheese

1. Sprinkle chicken with salt and pepper, if desired.

2. In large skillet, melt margarine over medium-high heat. Add chicken; cook 2 minutes on each side or until browned. Remove from skillet; set aside, reserving drippings. Keep warm.

3. In same skillet, sauté rice-vermicelli mix in reserved drippings over medium heat until vermicelli is golden brown. Stir in 2½ cups water, contents of seasoning packet and basil. Place chicken over rice mixture; bring to a boil over high heat.

Tomato, Basil & Broccoli Chicken

4. Cover; reduce heat. Simmer 15 minutes. Top with broccoli and tomato.

5. Cover; continue to simmer 5 minutes or until liquid is absorbed and chicken is no longer pink inside. Sprinkle with cheese. Cover; let stand a few minutes before serving.

Makes 4 servings

Sausage Corn Tart

   2 cups fresh corn kernels
   ½ pound hot Italian
      sausage
   1 small red bell pepper,
      diced
   1 green onion, sliced
   1 package prepared pie
      crust
   3 large eggs
   1 cup milk
   ¼ cup all-purpose flour
   1 teaspoon TABASCO®
      pepper sauce
   ½ teaspoon dry mustard
   ½ teaspoon salt

• In medium saucepan heat corn and enough water to cover; bring to boil. Reduce heat to low; cover and simmer 5 minutes until corn is tender. Drain.

• Remove casing from sausage. In large skillet over medium heat, cook sausage until well browned on all sides, stirring to break up sausage. With slotted spoon, remove sausage to plate.

• In drippings remaining in skillet, cook bell pepper 3 minutes; add green onion and cook 2 minutes longer, stirring occasionally.

• Preheat oven to 450°F. Line 10-inch fluted tart pan with removable bottom with prepared pie crust. Bake 10 minutes.

• In large bowl, beat eggs, milk, flour, TABASCO® sauce, mustard and salt until well blended. Stir in corn, sausage, bell pepper and green onion. Pour mixture into prepared pie crust.

• Reduce oven temperature to 350°F; bake tart 40 minutes or until knife inserted in center comes out clean.

Makes 6 servings

Penne with Fresh Herb Tomato Sauce

1 pound uncooked penne
    pasta
4 ripe large tomatoes,
    peeled and seeded*
½ cup tomato sauce
¼ cup FILIPPO BERIO®
    Olive Oil
1 to 2 tablespoons lemon
    juice
2 teaspoons minced fresh
    parsley *or* 1 teaspoon
    dried parsley
1 teaspoon minced fresh
    rosemary, oregano or
    thyme *or* 1 teaspoon
    dried Italian
    seasoning
    Salt and freshly ground
    black pepper
    Shavings of Parmesan
    cheese

*For chunkier sauce, reserve 1 peeled,
seeded tomato. Finely chop; stir into
sauce.*

Cook pasta according to
package directions until al
dente (tender but still firm).
Drain; transfer to large bowl.
Process tomatoes in blender or
food processor until smooth.
Add tomato sauce. While
machine is running, very
slowly add olive oil. Add lemon
juice, parsley and herbs.
Process briefly at high speed.
Spoon sauce over hot or room-
temperature pasta. Season to
taste with salt and pepper. Top
with cheese.

Makes 4 servings

Turkey Gyros

1 turkey tenderloin
    (8 ounces)
1½ teaspoons Greek
    seasoning
1 cucumber
⅔ cup plain nonfat yogurt
¼ cup finely chopped
    onion
2 teaspoons dried dill
    weed
2 teaspoons fresh lemon
    juice
1 teaspoon olive oil
4 pita breads
1½ cups washed and
    shredded romaine
    lettuce
1 tomato, thinly sliced
2 tablespoons crumbled
    feta cheese

continued on page 46

**Penne with Fresh Herb
Tomato Sauce**

44

Turkey Gyros, continued

1. Cut turkey tenderloin across the grain into ¼-inch slices. Place turkey slices on plate; lightly sprinkle both sides with Greek seasoning. Let stand 5 minutes.

2. Cut two thirds of cucumber into thin slices. Finely chop remaining cucumber. Combine chopped cucumber, yogurt, onion, dill weed and lemon juice in small bowl.

3. Heat olive oil in large skillet over medium heat until hot. Add turkey. Cook 2 minutes on each side or until cooked through. Wrap 2 pita breads in paper towel. Microwave at HIGH 30 seconds or just until warmed. Repeat with remaining pita breads.

4. Divide lettuce, tomato, cucumber slices, turkey, cheese and yogurt-cucumber sauce evenly among pita breads. Fold edges over and secure with wooden picks.

Makes 4 servings

Smorgasburgers

- 2 tablespoons vegetable oil, divided
- 1 medium onion, chopped
- 1 medium apple, peeled and chopped
- 1 clove garlic, minced
- 1 teaspoon dried sage *or* 1 tablespoon fresh chopped sage
- 1 pound ground turkey
- 3 cups cooked brown rice
- 2 tablespoons ketchup
- ½ teaspoon salt
- ¼ teaspoon ground black pepper
- 6 hamburger buns, toasted
- Assorted condiments

Heat 1 tablespoon oil in large skillet over medium-high heat until hot. Add onion, apple, garlic and sage; cook 3 to 5 minutes or until onion is tender. Remove from heat. Combine onion mixture, turkey, rice, ketchup, salt and pepper. Shape into patties. Heat remaining 1 tablespoon oil in same skillet over medium-high heat until hot. Cook burgers 6 minutes per side or until thoroughly cooked. Serve on buns with condiments.

Makes 6 servings

*Favorite recipe from **USA Rice Council***

Turkey Gyros

Savory Pork & Apple Stir-Fry

- 1 package (7.2 ounces) RICE-A-RONI® Rice Pilaf
- 1⅓ cups apple juice or apple cider
- 1 pound boneless pork loin, pork tenderloin or skinless, boneless chicken breast halves
- 1 teaspoon paprika
- 1 teaspoon dried thyme leaves
- ½ teaspoon ground sage or poultry seasoning
- ½ teaspoon salt (optional)
- 2 tablespoons margarine or butter
- 2 medium apples, cored, sliced
- 1 teaspoon cornstarch
- ⅓ cup coarsely chopped walnuts

1. Prepare Rice-A-Roni® as package directs, substituting 1 cup water and 1 cup apple juice for water in directions.

2. While Rice-A-Roni® is simmering, cut pork into 1½×¼-inch strips. Combine seasonings; toss with meat.

3. In second large skillet, melt margarine over medium heat.

Savory Pork & Apple Stir-Fry

Stir-fry meat 3 to 4 minutes or just until pork is no longer pink.

4. Add apples; stir-fry 2 to 3 minutes or until apples are almost tender. Add combined remaining ⅓ cup apple juice and cornstarch. Stir-fry 1 to 2 minutes or until thickened to form glaze.

5. Stir in nuts. Serve rice topped with pork mixture.

Makes 4 servings

Harvest Pizza

4 tablespoons WISH-BONE® Italian Dressing*

2 cups suggested fresh vegetables**

1 pound fresh or frozen (thawed) pizza or bread dough

1 cup (about 4 ounces) shredded mozzarella cheese

2 tablespoons grated Parmesan cheese

*Also terrific with Wish-Bone® Robusto Italian or Lite Italian Dressing.

**Suggested fresh vegetables: Use any combination of the following to equal 2 cups—sliced zucchini, yellow squash, tomatoes, eggplant, mushrooms, green beans, red, yellow or green peppers, asparagus cut into 2-inch pieces or snow peas.

• In 10-inch skillet, heat 2 tablespoons Italian dressing and cook suggested fresh vegetables over medium heat, stirring occasionally, 3 minutes or until crisp-tender; set aside.

• Preheat oven to 450°F. Divide dough and shape into 2 balls. In lightly oiled pizza pans or cookie sheets, press dough to form desired shapes. Brush each crust with 1 tablespoon Italian dressing. With slotted spoon, top each crust with ½ of the cooked vegetables and cheeses.

• Bake uncovered 18 minutes or until crusts are golden brown.

• Sprinkle, if desired, with sliced fresh basil or green onions and freshly ground black pepper.

Makes about 4 servings

Shrimp Primavera

8 ounces capelli d'angelo
(angel hair pasta),
preferably fresh
1½ pounds medium-size
fresh shrimp, shelled
and deveined, with
tails removed
4 teaspoons minced garlic
2 cups thin carrot sticks
(about 3 inches long)
2 cups thin strips red bell
peppers (about
3 inches long)
2 cups thinly sliced ripe
plum tomatoes
2 cups thin strips
zucchini (about
3 inches long)
½ teaspoon crushed red
pepper flakes
½ cup skim milk
12 ounces (2 cartons)
ALPINE LACE® Fat
Free Cream Cheese
with Garlic & Herbs
1 cup slivered fresh basil
leaves *or* 1 cup minced
fresh parsley plus
2 tablespoons dried
basil
Sprigs of fresh basil
(optional)

1. Cook the pasta according to package directions until al dente. Drain, place in a large shallow pasta bowl and keep warm.

2. Half-fill the same saucepan with water, bring to a boil and cook the shrimp just until pink. Toss with the pasta and keep warm.

3. Spray a large nonstick skillet with nonstick cooking spray and heat over medium-high heat for 1 minute. Add the garlic and sauté for 1 minute. Stir in the carrots, bell peppers, tomatoes, zucchini and red pepper flakes. Cook, stirring constantly, for 5 minutes or until carrots are crisp-tender. Toss with the pasta and shrimp.

4. In a small saucepan, bring the milk to a boil over medium heat. Add the cream cheese and stir until melted. Toss with the pasta mixture, then sprinkle with the basil. Garnish with basil sprigs, if you wish. Serve hot!

Makes 6 servings

Shrimp Primavera

Chicken Caesar

¾ cup olive oil
¼ cup lemon juice
¼ cup finely grated
  Parmesan cheese
1 can (2 ounces)
  anchovies, drained
  and chopped
1 clove garlic, minced
2 teaspoons Dijon
  mustard
½ teaspoon black pepper
  Salt
4 boneless skinless
  chicken breast halves
½ pound green beans,
  trimmed, cooked and
  cooled
6 to 8 small new potatoes,
  cooked, cooled and
  cut into quarters
¾ cup cooked fresh or
  thawed frozen corn
1 medium carrot, thinly
  sliced
10 to 12 cherry tomatoes,
  cut into halves
2 green onions, sliced
  Finely chopped parsley
  or basil

To make Caesar dressing, place first 7 ingredients in food processor or blender; process until smooth and creamy. Add salt to taste.

Place chicken in a shallow glass dish. Pour ¼ cup dressing over chicken; turn to coat. Let stand while preparing vegetables, or cover and refrigerate up to 4 hours. Place vegetables in a large bowl; toss with remaining dressing. Spoon onto serving plates. Season lightly with salt.

Oil hot grid to help prevent sticking. Grill chicken, on a covered grill, over medium KINGSFORD® briquets, 6 to 8 minutes until chicken is cooked through, turning once. Slice chicken crosswise and serve with vegetables. Sprinkle with parsley or basil. Serve immediately or at room temperature.

Makes 4 servings

Seafood Kabobs

24 large sea scallops
12 medium shrimp, shelled
  and deveined
1 can (8½ ounces) whole
  small artichoke
  hearts, drained and
  cut into halves
2 red or yellow bell
  peppers, cut into
  2-inch pieces
¼ cup olive or vegetable oil
¼ cup lime juice
  Lime slices and sage
  sprigs for garnish

Seafood Kabobs

Thread scallops, shrimp, artichoke hearts and peppers alternately on metal or bamboo skewers. (Soak bamboo skewers in water at least 20 minutes to keep them from burning.) Combine oil and lime juice in a small bowl; brush kabobs with lime mixture.

Oil hot grid to help prevent sticking. Grill kabobs, on an uncovered grill, over low KINGSFORD® briquets, 6 to 8 minutes. Halfway through cooking time, baste with lime mixture, then turn kabobs and continue grilling until scallops and shrimp firm up and turn opaque throughout. Remove kabobs from grill; baste with lime mixture. Garnish with lime slices and sage sprigs.

Makes 6 servings

Farmstand Vegetables & Sides

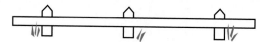

Fresh Vegetable Basil Medley

3 small zucchini squash
3 small yellow squash
2 medium carrots
4 teaspoons vegetable oil
2 teaspoons dried basil
　leaves
　Fresh basil leaves
　(optional)

Cut vegetables into julienne strips. Heat oil in large skillet over medium-high heat. Add carrots; cook 1 minute. Add zucchini, yellow squash and dried basil; cook and stir until vegetables are crisp-tender. Garnish with fresh basil, if desired. Serve hot. Refrigerate leftovers.

Makes 4 to 6 side-dish
servings

*Favorite recipe from **Bob Evans***
***Farms**®*

Fresh Vegetable Basil
Medley

Vegetable Risotto

1 cup fresh mushrooms,
   sliced
½ cup sliced zucchini
½ cup chopped bell pepper
½ cup chopped onion
1 teaspoon crushed dried
   basil
1 clove garlic, minced
2 teaspoons vegetable oil
1 cup uncooked
   RICELAND® Extra
   Long Grain Rice
1 (14½-ounce) can chicken
   broth
1½ cups water
½ cup grated Parmesan
   cheese

In 3-quart saucepan, sauté
mushrooms, zucchini, bell
pepper, onion, basil and garlic
in oil over medium heat for
3 minutes. Add rice and stir to
coat; cook for 2 more minutes.
Stir in half of broth, then
water; cook over medium heat
for 5 minutes or until broth is
absorbed. Stir in remaining
broth, then water; cook,
stirring constantly, until broth
is absorbed. When all of liquid
has been absorbed and rice is
tender, remove from heat and
stir in cheese.

Makes 6 servings

Vegetable Risotto

Twice-Baked Squash

2 acorn squash (about
    12 to 14 ounces each),
    cooked, halved and
    seeded
½ cup grated Parmesan
    cheese, divided
1 cup (8 ounces) low-fat
    (1%) cottage cheese
2 eggs
½ cup instant mashed
    potato flakes
½ cup minced green
    onions with tops
1 teaspoon lemon juice
1 teaspoon salt
⅓ cup unseasoned
    croutons or stuffing
    cubes

Scoop pulp from squash and mash in large bowl, reserving shells. Reserve 2 tablespoons Parmesan cheese; beat remaining ingredients except croutons into mashed squash until thoroughly blended. Spoon mixture into reserved shells. Sprinkle with reserved Parmesan cheese and croutons. Place in shallow baking pan.

Bake in preheated 350°F oven until knife inserted near centers comes out clean, about 35 to 40 minutes.

Makes 4 servings

*Favorite recipe from **American Egg Board***

Wild Roasted Medley

1 cup *each*, diced:
    zucchini, fennel bulb,
    carrot, celery, onion
    and peeled potato
    (about 4 ounces each)
⅓ cup olive oil
3 to 4 cloves garlic,
    minced
    Salt and pepper to taste
2 large tomatoes, peeled,
    seeded and chopped
1 teaspoon sugar
2 tablespoons snipped
    fresh dill
2 tablespoons minced
    fresh cilantro
3 cups cooked wild rice

Preheat oven to 450°F. In large bowl, combine vegetables (except tomatoes), oil, garlic, salt and pepper. Place tomatoes in bottom of large baking dish; sprinkle with sugar. Top with vegetable mixture; cook 20 minutes. Remove from oven; stir in dill and cilantro. Cook 10 to 15 minutes longer. Stir in wild rice; adjust seasonings if necessary. Serve warm or at room temperature, or cover and refrigerate one day to allow flavors to blend. Reheat before serving.

Makes 6 to 8 servings

*Favorite recipe from **Minnesota Cultivated Wild Rice Council***

Grilled Vegetables with Balsamic Vinaigrette

1 medium eggplant
    (about 1¼ pounds)
2 medium zucchini
2 to 3 medium yellow
    squash
2 medium red bell
    peppers
¾ cup olive oil
¼ cup balsamic vinegar
1 teaspoon salt
¼ teaspoon black pepper
1 clove garlic, minced
2 to 3 tablespoons finely
    chopped mixed fresh
    herbs

Trim and slice eggplant, zucchini and yellow squash lengthwise into ¼- to ½-inch-thick slices. Core, seed and cut red peppers into 1-inch-wide strips. Place vegetables in a deep serving platter or wide shallow casserole. Combine oil, vinegar, salt, black pepper, garlic and chopped herbs in a small bowl. Pour vinaigrette over vegetables; turn to coat. Let stand 30 minutes or longer. Lift vegetables from vinaigrette, leaving vinaigrette that doesn't cling to the vegetables in the dish. Oil hot grid to help prevent sticking. Grill vegetables, on covered grill, over medium KINGSFORD® briquets, 8 to 16 minutes until fork-tender, turning once or twice. (Time will depend on the vegetable; eggplant takes the longest.) As vegetables are done, return them to the platter and then turn to coat with vinaigrette. (Or, cut eggplant, zucchini and yellow squash into cubes, then toss with red peppers and vinaigrette.) Serve warm or at room temperature.

Makes 6 servings

Peas with Cukes 'n' Dill

½ medium cucumber,
    peeled and seeded
2 tablespoons margarine
    or butter
2 pounds fresh peas,
    shelled *or* 1 package
    (10 ounce) frozen
    peas, thawed
1 teaspoon dried dill weed

1. Cut cucumber into ¼-inch slices. Heat margarine in medium skillet over medium-high heat until melted and bubbly. Add peas and cucumber. Cook and stir 5 minutes until vegetables are crisp-tender.

2. Stir in dill weed and season to taste with salt and pepper.

Makes 4 side-dish servings

**Grilled Vegetables with
Balsamic Vinaigrette**

Italian-Style Roasted Peppers

Italian-Style Roasted Peppers

**6 large red, green or
    yellow bell peppers**
**1 cup (8 ounces) WISH-
    BONE® Italian or Lite
    Italian Dressing**
**½ cup chopped fresh basil
    leaves *or* 1 tablespoon
    dried basil leaves**
**⅛ teaspoon ground black
    pepper**

In large aluminum foil-lined baking pan or on broiler rack, place bell peppers. Broil, turning occasionally, 20 minutes or until peppers turn almost completely black. Immediately place in paper bag; close bag and let cool about 30 minutes. Under cold running water, peel off skin and remove stems and seeds; slice peppers into long, thick strips.

In large bowl, combine bell peppers with remaining ingredients. Cover and marinate in refrigerator at least 4 hours, stirring occasionally. For best flavor, serve bell peppers at room temperature and, if desired, with olives, mozzarella cheese and tomatoes.

*Makes about 3 cups
roasted peppers*

Baked Tomatoes with BEL PAESE®

3 to 4 large ripe tomatoes, cut into halves
1 to 2 ounces BEL PAESE® semi-soft cheese, cut into small cubes
2 anchovy fillets, mashed
1 tablespoon capers
2 to 3 fresh parsley sprigs, minced
1 tablespoon extra virgin olive oil

Grease 12×8-inch microwavable dish. Remove and reserve tomato pulp from tomatoes, discarding seeds and juice. Place tomato halves in prepared baking dish.

Chop tomato pulp and combine with cheese, anchovies, capers and parsley in small bowl. Fill tomato halves with tomato-cheese mixture. Drizzle olive oil over tomatoes. Microwave on HIGH for 5 to 10 minutes until hot and cheese melts, turning dish halfway through cooking time.

Makes 6 to 8 servings

Zucchini-Barley Mexicali

Vegetable oil cooking spray
1 teaspoon olive oil
1 cup cubed onion
2 small cloves garlic, minced
2 cups cubed zucchini (about 1 pound)
1 cup fresh California Tomatoes, cubed (about 1 pound or 3 large)
1 cup cooked barley
1 tablespoon chopped fresh parsley
¼ teaspoon chili powder
1 cup shredded, fat-free sharp Cheddar cheese

Preheat oven to 350°F. Coat medium nonstick skillet with cooking spray. Heat skillet over medium heat; add oil. When hot, add onion and garlic; sauté 1 minute. Stir in zucchini and tomatoes; continue to cook and stir until vegetables are crisp-tender. Stir in barley, parsley and chili powder. Spoon mixture into 1-quart baking dish coated with cooking spray; sprinkle with cheese. Bake 10 to 15 minutes or until cheese melts. *Makes 4 servings*

*Favorite recipe from **California Tomato Commission***

Barbecued Corn with Three Savory Butters

12 ears corn, unhusked
Three Savory Butters
(recipes follow)

Carefully peel back husks; remove corn silk. Bring husks up and tie securely with kitchen string. Soak corn covered in cold water for 30 minutes.

Place corn on grid. Grill over medium-high coals 25 minutes or until corn is tender, turning often. Remove string and husks. Serve with your choice of savory butter.

Makes 12 side-dish servings

Prep Time: 40 minutes
Cook Time: 25 minutes

Horseradish Butter

½ cup (1 stick) butter or
margarine, softened
3 tablespoons FRENCH'S®
Deli Brown Mustard
1 tablespoon horseradish

Red Hot Chili Butter

½ cup (1 stick) butter or
margarine, softened
2 tablespoons FRANK'S®
Original REDHOT®
Cayenne Pepper
Sauce
1 teaspoon chili powder
1 clove garlic, minced

Herb Butter

½ cup (1 stick) butter or
margarine, softened
2 tablespoons snipped
fresh chives
1 tablespoon FRENCH'S®
Worcestershire Sauce
1 tablespoon minced fresh
parsley
½ teaspoon dried thyme
leaves
½ teaspoon salt (optional)

Place ingredients for each flavored butter in separate small bowl; beat until smooth. Serve at room temperature with hot corn.

Makes about ½ cup each

Barbecued Corn with Three Savory Butters

Layered Vegetable Bake

2 slices day-old white
   bread, crumbled
2 tablespoons chopped
   fresh parsley
   (optional)
2 tablespoons margarine
   or butter, melted
1 large all-purpose potato
   (about 8 ounces),
   thinly sliced
1 large yellow or red bell
   pepper, sliced
1 envelope LIPTON®
   Recipe Secrets®
   Savory Herb with
   Garlic or Golden
   Onion Soup Mix
1 large tomato, sliced

Preheat oven to 375°F.

Spray 1½-quart round casserole or baking dish with nonstick cooking spray. In small bowl, combine bread crumbs, parsley and margarine; set aside.

In prepared baking dish, arrange potato slices; top with yellow pepper. Sprinkle with savory herb with garlic soup mix. Arrange tomato slices over pepper, overlapping slightly. Sprinkle with bread crumb mixture. Cover with aluminum foil and bake 45 minutes. Remove foil and continue baking 15 minutes or until vegetables are tender.

Makes about 6 servings

Zucchini Casserole with BEL PAESE®

3 to 4 medium zucchini,
   cut lengthwise into
   ¼-inch slices
4 to 5 ounces BEL
   PAESE® semi-soft
   cheese, thinly sliced
2 to 3 large ripe tomatoes,
   chopped
2 to 3 fresh basil leaves,
   minced *or* ½ teaspoon
   dried basil leaves

Arrange half of zucchini in 9-inch square microwavable dish. Cover with half of cheese slices. Top with half of tomatoes and basil. Repeat layers. Microwave on HIGH for 15 minutes, turning dish halfway through cooking time.

Makes 4 servings

Layered Vegetable Bake

Oven-Roasted Vegetables

**1½ pounds assorted fresh
vegetables***
**1 envelope LIPTON®
Recipe Secrets®
Savory Herb with
Garlic Soup Mix****
**2 tablespoons olive or
vegetable oil*****

**Use any combination of the following
vegetables, sliced: zucchini, yellow
squash, red, green or yellow bell
peppers, carrots, celery or mushrooms.*

***Also terrific with Lipton® Recipe
Secrets® Golden Herb with Lemon,
Italian Herb with Tomato, Onion or
Golden Onion Soup Mix.*

****Substitution: Spray pan lightly with
nonstick cooking spray and replace oil
with 2 tablespoons water.*

Preheat oven to 450°F.

In large plastic bag or bowl,
place all ingredients. Close bag
and shake or toss in bowl until
vegetables are evenly coated.
In 13×9-inch baking or
roasting pan, arrange
vegetables; discard bag. Bake,
uncovered, 20 minutes or until
vegetables are tender, stirring
once.

*Makes about 4 (½-cup)
servings*

Garden Fresh Vegetable and Herb Rice

**1 (16-ounce) can fat-free
chicken broth with
⅓ less salt**
**1 cup uncooked
RICELAND® Extra
Long Grain Rice**
1 cup sliced zucchini
**1 cup fresh or frozen
whole kernel corn**
½ teaspoon salt
⅛ teaspoon pepper
**1 medium tomato,
chopped**
**⅓ cup chopped green
onions**
**1 tablespoon chopped
fresh basil *or*
1 teaspoon dried basil
leaves**

In medium saucepan, combine
chicken broth, rice, zucchini,
corn, salt and pepper. Bring to
a boil over high heat; reduce
heat to low. Cover; simmer
15 minutes. Stir in tomato,
green onions and basil.

Makes 6 servings

Oven-Roasted Vegetables

Fruit Basket Desserts & More

Mapley Berry Shortcake

1 cup blueberries
1 cup sliced strawberries
½ cup LOG CABIN® Syrup,
    divided
1 cup whipping (heavy)
    cream
4 sponge cake dessert
    shells

MIX berries and 3 tablespoons of the syrup in small bowl. Let stand 15 minutes.

BEAT cream and ¼ cup of the syrup in medium bowl with electric mixer on medium speed until soft peaks form.

BRUSH dessert shells lightly with remaining 1 tablespoon syrup. Top with berry mixture and whipped cream. Serve immediately. Store leftover dessert in refrigerator.

Makes 4 servings

Prep Time: 30 minutes

Mapley Berry Shortcake

Country Fruit Pie

2 pie crust sticks
5 fresh California peaches
    or nectarines, each
    cut into 8 slices (about
    3 cups)
3 fresh California plums,
    each cut into 6 slices
    (about 1 cup)
⅓ cup honey
3 tablespoons all-purpose
    flour
½ teaspoon almond
    extract

Preheat oven to 400°F. Roll out
1 pie crust stick according to
package directions to fit 8-inch
pie dish. Roll out remaining
pie crust stick; cut out about
35 leaf shapes with leaf cutter.
Gently toss fruit, honey, flour
and almond extract in large
bowl. Spoon fruit mixture into
crust. Place 8 leaf cut-outs
over fruit; press remaining
leaves onto rim of pie crust
with small amount of water.
Bake 25 to 30 minutes or until
crust is browned and fruit is
easily pierced with knife.

Makes 8 servings

*Favorite recipe from **California Tree
Fruit Agreement***

Low-Fat Harvest Apple Crumb Tart

1 (3-ounce) package split
    ladyfingers
¼ cup light brown sugar
¼ cup rolled oats
2 teaspoons all-purpose
    flour
1 teaspoon pumpkin pie
    spice
1 teaspoon grated lemon
    peel
1 cup (4 ounces) shredded
    GJETOST cheese
1 cup natural applesauce
    (no sugar added)
½ cup apple butter (no
    sugar added)
½ cup currants or raisins
4 cups Granny Smith or
    other firm cooking
    apples, peeled, cored
    and cut into large
    chunks
¼ cup granulated sugar
2 teaspoons cinnamon

Preheat oven to 350°F. Spray
11-inch tart pan with cooking
spray. Line pan with
ladyfingers, split side facing
up. (Pan will not be completely
covered.) Set aside.

For crumb topping, combine brown sugar, oats, flour, pumpkin pie spice and lemon peel in medium bowl; mix well. Blend in cheese with fingers until mixture resembles coarse meal; set aside.

For filling, combine applesauce, apple butter and currants in small bowl; set aside. Spray large skillet generously with cooking spray. Cook apples, granulated sugar and cinnamon over high heat 8 minutes, stirring frequently. Spoon apple mixture evenly into prepared tart pan. Spread applesauce mixture evenly over apples; sprinkle evenly with crumb topping.

Bake tart 30 minutes. Serve warm, at room temperature or chilled with additional shredded Gjetost cheese and nonfat frozen yogurt, if desired.

Makes 8 to 10 servings

Low-Fat Harvest Apple Crumb Tart

Fantasy in Berries

1 bag (12 ounces) frozen
  unsweetened
  raspberries, thawed
¼ cup plus 2 tablespoons
  sugar, divided
1 tablespoon fresh lemon
  juice
2 cups sliced fresh
  strawberries
1 cup fresh raspberries
1 cup fresh blueberries
1 cup low-fat ricotta
  cheese
1 teaspoon vanilla extract
¼ teaspoon almond
  extract

1. To prepare raspberry sauce, place thawed frozen raspberries, ¼ cup sugar and lemon juice in blender or food processor; blend until smooth. Pour through strainer to remove seeds. Spoon 3 tablespoons raspberry sauce on each of 8 plates. Tilt each plate, rotating to spread raspberry sauce over bottom of plate.

2. Arrange ¼ cup sliced strawberries, 2 tablespoons fresh raspberries and 2 tablespoons fresh blueberries on top of sauce in desired pattern on each plate.

3. Place cheese, remaining 2 tablespoons sugar and vanilla and almond extracts in clean blender or food processor; blend until smooth and satiny. Spoon cheese mixture into pastry bag and pipe onto berries, using about 2 tablespoons per serving. (Use star tip to make rosettes or various sizes of writing tips to drizzle mixture over berries.) Before serving, garnish with mint sprigs and edible flowers, such as pansies, violets or nasturtiums, if desired.

Makes 8 servings

Fresh Fruit Baskets

3 tablespoons apple jelly
½ teaspoon lemon juice
½ teaspoon vanilla extract
1 cup mixed cut-up fresh
  fruit
1 package ATHENS® Mini
  Fillo Dough Shells

In small saucepan, melt apple jelly over low heat. Remove from heat and stir in lemon juice and vanilla; cool slightly. Combine mixed fruit and jelly mixture, stirring just until fruit is glazed. Spoon fruit into shells and serve immediately.

Makes 15 fruit baskets

Fantasy in Berries

Peach Delight Pie

Filling

2½ cups sliced, peeled
    peaches (about
    1¼ pounds or 2 to
    3 large)
¾ cup granulated sugar
¼ cup quick-cooking
    tapioca
1 teaspoon lemon juice
1 teaspoon peach-flavored
    brandy

Crumb Mixture

¼ cup all-purpose flour
¼ cup packed brown sugar
¼ cup chopped almonds
3 tablespoons butter or
    margarine, melted

Crust

1 (9-inch) Classic CRISCO®
    Double Crust (page 76)

Glaze

1 egg white, slightly
    beaten
Granulated sugar

1. For Filling, combine peaches, ¾ cup granulated sugar, tapioca, lemon juice and brandy in medium bowl. Stir well. Let stand while making Crumb Mixture and Crust.

2. For Crumb Mixture, combine flour, brown sugar, almonds and butter. Mix until crumbly. Heat oven to 425°F.

3. For Crust, prepare as directed on page 76. Roll and press bottom crust into 9-inch pie plate. *Do not bake.* Sprinkle half of Crumb Mixture over unbaked pie crust. Add Filling. Top with remaining Crumb Mixture.

4. Cut out desired shapes from top crust with cookie cutter. Place on filling around edge of pie.

5. For Glaze, brush cutouts with egg white. Sprinkle with granulated sugar. Cover edge of pie with foil to prevent overbrowning.

6. Bake at 425°F for 10 minutes. *Reduce oven temperature to 350°F.* Bake 25 minutes. Remove foil. Bake 5 minutes. Serve barely warm or at room temperature.

Makes 1 (9-inch) pie

Peach Delight Pie

9-inch Classic CRISCO® Double Crust

2 cups all-purpose flour
1 teaspoon salt
¾ CRISCO® Stick *or* ¾ cup CRISCO® all-vegetable shortening
5 tablespoons cold water

1. Spoon flour into measuring cup and level. Combine flour and salt in medium bowl.

2. Cut in shortening using pastry blender or 2 knives until flour is blended to form pea-size chunks.

3. Sprinkle with water, 1 tablespoon at a time. Toss lightly with fork until dough forms a ball.

4. Divide dough in half. Press half of dough between hands to form a 5- to 6-inch "pancake." Flour rolling surface and rolling pin lightly. Roll dough into circle. Trim circle 1 inch larger than upside-down pie plate. Carefully remove trimmed dough. Set aside to reroll and use for pastry cutout garnish, if desired. Repeat with remaining half of dough.

Makes 2 (9-inch) crusts

Blueberry Cheesecake

2 (8-ounce) packages PHILADELPHIA BRAND® Cream Cheese, softened
½ cup sugar
½ teaspoon vanilla
2 eggs
1 cup blueberries, divided
1 (6-ounce or 9-inch) KEEBLER READY CRUST™ Graham Cracker Pie Crust

1. MIX cream cheese, sugar and vanilla at medium speed with electric mixer until well blended. Add eggs; mix until blended. Stir in ½ cup blueberries.

2. POUR into crust. Sprinkle with remaining ½ cup blueberries.

3. BAKE at 350°F, 40 minutes or until center is almost set. Cool. Refrigerate 3 hours or overnight. Garnish with COOL WHIP® Whipped Topping and additional blueberries.

Makes 8 servings

Prep Time: 10 minutes
Cook Time: 40 minutes

Chocolate Dipped or Drizzled Fruit

About 36 strawberries,
    orange segments, kiwi
    slices, pineapple
    chunks, pretzels,
    marshmallows, cake
    cubes or whole nuts
1 cup (6 ounces) NESTLÉ®
    TOLL HOUSE® Semi-
    Sweet Chocolate
    Morsels
2 tablespoons shortening

RINSE fruit; pat dry. Melt morsels and shortening over hot (not boiling) water, stirring until smooth. Remove from heat; cool slightly. Dip fruit about halfway into chocolate mixture; shake off excess. Or, drizzle chocolate from pastry bag fitted with small tip, a heavy-duty plastic bag with tiny corner snipped off, or squeeze bottle with small tip. Place chocolate-dipped pieces on waxed paper-lined tray; chill for 15 minutes or until coating is set.

Makes about 3 dozen pieces

Microwave Directions:
MICROWAVE morsels and shortening in microwave-safe bowl on HIGH (100%) power for 1 minute; stir. Microwave at additional 10- to 20-second intervals, stirring until smooth. Cool and dip as directed.

Other Coatings:
MICROWAVE Nestlé® Toll House® Milk Chocolate, Butterscotch or Premier White Morsels as directed using MEDIUM-HIGH (70%) power.

Tiger Cookie Pie

1 package (20 ounces)
    refrigerated oatmeal
    or chocolate chip
    cookie dough
1 quart vanilla ice cream
4 fresh California
    nectarines, sliced
½ teaspoon ground
    cinnamon

Preheat oven to 350°F. Spread cookie dough on bottom of 10-inch pie pan. Bake 18 to 20 minutes or until brown. Cool completely; freeze crust until firm. Remove ice cream from freezer; let soften 30 minutes. Spread ice cream over cookie layer, flattening top. Return pie to freezer. Toss nectarines with cinnamon in medium bowl. Arrange nectarines over ice cream layer. Cut and serve immediately.

Makes 8 servings

*Favorite recipe from **California Tree Fruit Agreement***

Fresh Berry Cobbler Cake

1 pint fresh berries
(blueberries,
blackberries,
raspberries and/or
strawberries)
1 cup all-purpose flour
1¼ cups sugar, divided
1 teaspoon baking powder
¼ teaspoon salt
3 tablespoons butter or
margarine
½ cup milk
1 tablespoon cornstarch
1 cup cold water
Additional berries
(optional)

Preheat oven to 375°F. Place berries in 9×9-inch baking pan; set aside. Combine flour, ½ cup sugar, baking powder and salt in large bowl. Cut in butter with pastry blender or two knives until coarse crumbs form. Stir in milk. Spoon over berries. Combine remaining ¾ cup sugar and cornstarch in small bowl. Stir in water until sugar mixture dissolves; pour over berry mixture. Bake 35 to 40 minutes or until lightly browned. Serve warm or cool completely. Garnish with additional berries, if desired.

Makes 6 servings

Favorite recipe from **Bob Evans Farms**®

Chocolate Dipped Strawberry Petites

¾ cup frozen whipped
topping, thawed
1 package ATHENS® Mini
Fillo Dough Shells
15 small strawberries,
stems removed
½ cup semisweet
chocolate chips

Spoon or pipe whipped topping into shells, filling about three-fourths full. Rinse and dry strawberries. Melt chocolate chips in microwave on MEDIUM (50% power) for 2 minutes; stir until smooth. Holding stem end, dip strawberry halfway into melted chocolate; place on top of prepared shells and serve immediately.

Makes 15 petites

Tips: For thinner coating, add 1 teaspoon shortening to chocolate when melting.

For extra flavor, blend ½ teaspoon brandy, strawberry extract or vanilla extract into whipped topping before filling shells.

For variety, dip shells in chocolate instead of dipping strawberries.

Fresh Berry Cobbler Cake

Nectarine-Pecan Breakfast Muffins

1½ cups whole wheat flour
½ cup chopped pecans
¼ cup packed brown sugar
2 teaspoons baking powder
½ teaspoon salt
½ teaspoon ground nutmeg
1½ fresh California nectarines, chopped (1 cup)
1 cup low-fat milk
1 egg, beaten
3 tablespoons vegetable oil
12 pecan halves for garnish

Preheat oven to 400°F. Grease 12 (2½-inch) muffin cups; set aside.

Combine flour, pecans, brown sugar, baking powder, salt and nutmeg in large bowl. Combine nectarines, milk, egg and oil in medium bowl until well blended; stir into flour mixture just until moistened. (Batter will be thick and lumpy.) Spoon evenly into prepared muffin cups. Place pecan half on top of each muffin.

Nectarine-Pecan Breakfast Muffins

Bake 20 minutes or until golden brown and wooden toothpick inserted in centers of muffins comes out clean. Remove from pan; cool on wire rack 10 minutes. Serve warm or cool completely.

Makes 12 muffins

Favorite recipe from **California Tree Fruit Agreement**

Pears Wrapped in Fillo

½ **cup golden raisins**
½ **cup chopped dried apricots**
¼ **cup amaretto, warmed**
6 **medium Bartlett pears**
2 **cups water**
   Juice of 1 lemon
3 **ounces cream cheese, softened**
1 **tablespoon brown sugar**
¼ **cup sliced almonds, toasted**
¼ **cup butter, softened**
7 **sheets ATHENS® or APOLLO® Fillo Dough**

In small bowl combine raisins, apricots and amaretto. Let stand for 20 minutes.

Peel pears, leaving stems intact. Scoop core of pear out from bottom with melon baller. Trim pear so bottom is flat. Combine water and lemon juice in large bowl; add pears to prevent them from browning.

In medium bowl combine cream cheese, sugar and almonds. Fold in raisin mixture. Remove pears from water. Fill each pear core with cream cheese-raisin mixture.

Butter and layer 4 fillo sheets and cut stack into 6 squares. Place 1 pear on each square and gather sides of fillo up around pear. Brush remaining 3 fillo sheets with butter on one half of each sheet (lengthwise). Fold sheets in half lengthwise and cut lengthwise into 1-inch strips. Starting at top of pear, wrap fillo strip around pear, overlapping strips slightly. Brush with butter and place on cookie sheet.

Bake in preheated 375°F oven for 30 minutes or until golden brown. Garnish pears with amaretto-flavored whipped cream, raspberry sauce and/or chocolate sauce.

Makes 6 servings

Country Apple Rhubarb Pie

Crust

1 (9-inch) Classic
    CRISCO® Double
    Crust (page 76)

Filling

9 cups sliced, peeled
    Granny Smith apples
    (about 3 pounds or
    6 large apples)
1½ cups chopped (about
    ½-inch pieces) fresh
    rhubarb, peeled if
    tough
¾ cup granulated sugar
½ cup firmly packed light
    brown sugar
2 tablespoons all-purpose
    flour
1 tablespoon cornstarch
1 teaspoon ground
    cinnamon
¼ teaspoon freshly grated
    nutmeg

Glaze

1 egg, beaten
1 tablespoon water
1 tablespoon granulated
    sugar
1 teaspoon ground pecans
    or walnuts
⅛ teaspoon ground
    cinnamon

1. For crust, prepare as directed. Roll and press bottom crust into 9- or 9½-inch deep-dish pie plate. *Do not bake.* Heat oven to 425°F.

2. For filling, combine apples and rhubarb in large bowl. Combine ¾ cup granulated sugar, brown sugar, flour, cornstarch, 1 teaspoon cinnamon and nutmeg in medium bowl. Sprinkle over fruit. Toss to coat. Spoon into unbaked pie crust. Moisten pastry edge with water. Cover pie with lattice top, cutting strips 1 inch wide. Flute edge high.

3. For glaze, combine egg and water in small bowl. Brush over crust. Combine remaining glaze ingredients in small bowl. Sprinkle over crust.

4. Bake at 425°F for 20 minutes. *Reduce oven temperature to 350°F.* Bake 30 to 40 minutes or until filling in center is bubbly and crust is golden brown. Place sheet of foil or baking sheet under pie if it starts to bubble over. Cool to room temperature.

Makes 1 (9-inch or 9½-inch)
deep-dish pie

Country Apple Rhubarb Pie

The Harvest Pantry

Zucchini Chow Chow

2 cups thinly sliced
    zucchini
2 cups thinly sliced yellow
    summer squash*
½ cup thinly sliced red
    onion
    Salt
1½ cups cider vinegar
1 to 1¼ cups sugar
1½ tablespoons pickling
    spice
1 cup thinly sliced carrots
1 small red bell pepper,
    thinly sliced

*If yellow summer squash is not
available, increase zucchini to 4 cups.*

1. Sprinkle zucchini, summer squash and onion lightly with salt; let stand in colander 30 minutes. Rinse well with cold water; drain thoroughly. Pat dry with paper towels.

2. Combine vinegar, sugar and pickling spice in medium saucepan. Bring to a boil over high heat. Add carrots and bell pepper; bring to a boil. Remove from heat; cool to room temperature.

3. Spoon zucchini, summer squash, onion and carrot mixture into sterilized jars; cover and refrigerate up to 3 weeks.

Makes 24 (¼-cup) servings

Zucchini Chow Chow

Herbed Vinegar

**1 bottle (12 ounces) white
wine vinegar (1½ cups)
½ cup fresh basil leaves**

Pour vinegar into
nonaluminum medium
saucepan. Heat until very hot,
stirring occasionally. *Do not
boil.* (If vinegar boils, it will
become cloudy.)

Pour into glass bowl; add basil.
Cover with plastic wrap. Let
stand in cool place about
1 week until desired amount of
flavor develops. Strain before
using. Store up to 6 months in
jar or bottle with tight-fitting
lid.   *Makes about 1½ cups*

Variations: Substitute
1 tablespoon fresh oregano,
thyme, chervil or tarragon for
basil. Or, substitute cider
vinegar for wine vinegar.

Raspberry Vinegar

**1 bottle (12 ounces) white
wine vinegar (1½ cups)
½ cup sugar
1 cup fresh raspberries or
sliced strawberries,
crushed**

Combine vinegar and sugar in
nonaluminum medium
saucepan. Heat until very hot,
stirring occasionally. *Do not
boil.* (If vinegar boils, it will
become cloudy.)

Pour into glass bowl; stir in
raspberries. Cover with plastic
wrap. Let stand in cool place
about 1 week until desired
amount of flavor develops.
Strain through fine-meshed
sieve or cheesecloth twice.
Store in refrigerator up to
6 months in jar or bottle with
tight-fitting lid.
          Makes about 2 cups

Left to right:
**Herbed Vinegar and
Raspberry Vinegar**

Spicy Red Pepper Jelly

2 large red bell peppers,
cut into pieces (about
4 cups)
1 small onion, cut into
6 pieces (about 1 cup)
1½ cups cider vinegar,
divided
6½ cups sugar
1 (3-ounce) pouch liquid
pectin
3 to 4 teaspoons
TABASCO® pepper
sauce

Place bell peppers, onion and ¼ cup vinegar in food processor; process until finely chopped. Scrape mixture into large, heavy nonaluminum pot. Add remaining 1¼ cups vinegar; bring to a boil over high heat. Reduce heat to low; simmer 5 minutes until mixture is slightly thickened, stirring occasionally. Stir in sugar; increase heat to high and bring to a boil, stirring constantly. Boil 1 minute, stirring constantly. (Be careful, as jam tends to boil over and is *very* hot. Reduce heat slightly, if necessary.) Remove from heat; stir in pectin until completely blended. Skim off foam that rises to surface. Stir in TABASCO® sauce to taste.

Ladle jam into hot sterilized jars (½-pint size are best), leaving ¼-inch headspace. Wipe inside and outside rims clean with damp paper towel. Seal with sterilized new 2-piece lids, following manufacturer's instructions. Cool jars on wire rack. Store in cool place up to 6 months. Once opened, keep refrigerated.   *Makes 7 cups*

Strawberry Jam

6 cups mashed
strawberries (about
4 pints)
5 cups sugar
2 tablespoons bottled
lemon juice

Combine strawberries and sugar in large saucepan. Bring to a boil and cook to jelly stage (220°F), about 20 minutes, stirring constantly. Add lemon juice several minutes before cooking is complete. Immediately fill hot sterilized half-pint jars with jam, leaving ¼-inch headspace. Wipe jar tops and threads clean. Place hot lids on jars and screw bands on firmly. Process in boiling water canner 5 minutes.

Makes 5 to 6 half-pints

*Favorite recipe from **Alltrista Corporation Kerr Brand**®*

All-Purpose Plum Sauce

2 pounds fresh California
  plums, quartered
2½ cups sugar
½ cup vinegar
3 tablespoons soy sauce
1 teaspoon ground ginger
1/16 to ⅛ teaspoon ground
  red pepper

Combine all ingredients in large saucepan or Dutch oven. Bring to a boil over high heat; reduce heat to medium-low and cook about 10 minutes or until fruit is very tender. Remove from heat; purée mixture in blender. Return plum sauce to saucepan; cook 30 minutes longer or until thickened (215°F). Skim sauce to remove foam. Pour into clean hot jars; seal immediately. Process in boiling water bath for 15 minutes, if desired. Cool. Serve with sirloin strips (see below), broiled chicken or fish.

Makes 1 quart

Serving Suggestion: Cut 1 pound beef sirloin into long, thin strips; thread meat on skewers. Brush with plum sauce; broil 5 to 7 minutes, turning once. Serve with additional sauce.

*Favorite recipe from **California Tree Fruit Agreement***

Chunky Applesauce

10 tart apples (about
  3 pounds), peeled,
  cored and chopped
¾ cup packed light brown
  sugar
½ cup apple juice or apple
  cider
1½ teaspoons ground
  cinnamon
⅛ teaspoon salt
⅛ teaspoon ground
  nutmeg

1. Combine apples, brown sugar, apple juice, cinnamon, salt and nutmeg in heavy, large saucepan. Cover and cook over medium-low heat 40 to 45 minutes or until apples are tender, stirring occasionally with wooden spoon to break apples into chunks. Remove saucepan from heat. Cool completely.

2. Store in airtight container in refrigerator up to 1 month.

Makes about 5½ cups

Eggplant Chutney

2 large eggplants
    (2½ pounds),
    unpeeled, cut into
    ½-inch cubes
1 small onion, finely
    chopped
3 tablespoons minced
    garlic
3 tablespoons minced
    fresh ginger
3 tablespoons firmly
    packed light brown
    sugar
1 teaspoon dried
    rosemary leaves
1 teaspoon dried anise or
    fennel seeds
½ teaspoon dried thyme
    leaves
2 tablespoons balsamic
    vinegar
1 tablespoon Oriental
    sesame oil
¼ cup dark raisins
½ cup reduced-sodium
    chicken broth
2 tablespoons coarsely
    chopped walnuts

1. Preheat oven to 450°F. Arrange eggplant on 15×10-inch jelly-roll pan lined with foil. Add onion, garlic, ginger, brown sugar, rosemary, anise and thyme; toss to combine. Drizzle with vinegar and oil; stir to coat. Bake 1½ hours or until eggplant is browned and shriveled, stirring every 30 minutes.

2. Stir raisins into eggplant mixture and drizzle with chicken broth; bake 10 minutes or until broth is absorbed. Remove from oven; stir in walnuts. Cool. Serve on crackers or lavash as an appetizer, or serve warm or at room temperature as a condiment with roasted meats and poultry, if desired. Garnish with kale and orange slices, if desired. Store chutney in airtight container up to 10 days in refrigerator or 3 months in freezer.

Makes about 2¾ cups

Eggplant Chutney

Acknowledgments

The publisher would like to thank the companies and organizations listed below for the use of their recipes and photographs in this publication.

Alpine Lace Brands, Inc.

Alltrista Corporation Kerr Brand®

American Egg Board

American Spice Trade Association

Athens Foods®

Bob Evans Farms®

Buckeye Beans & Herbs

California Tomato Commission

California Tree Fruit Agreement

Cucina Classica Italiana, Inc.

Delmarva Poultry Industry, Inc.

Diamond Walnut Growers, Inc.

Filippo Berio Olive Oil

Golden Grain/Mission Pasta

The Kingsford Products Company

Kraft Foods, Inc.

Lawry's® Foods, Inc.

Lipton

McIlhenny Company

Minnesota Cultivated Wild Rice Council

Nestlé Food Company

Norseland, Inc.

The Procter & Gamble Company

Reckitt & Colman Inc.

RED•STAR® Yeast & Products, A Division of Universal Foods Corporation

Riceland Foods, Inc.

USA Rice Council

Wisconsin Milk Marketing Board

Index